"Billions of people follow Christ's teaching
and find in him the guiding light for their lives.
I am one of them…"

QUEEN ELIZABETH II
Christmas message, 2015

"There is only one person that the queen addresses as 'Your Majesty', and in this wonderful book we discover who that is and why she does that."
ALISTAIR BEGG, Senior Pastor, Parkside Church, Cleveland; Bible Teacher, Truth for Life

"This excellent children's book tells the story of a wonderful woman, Queen Elizabeth. She is a shining example of how God can guide and help us when we seek to follow him and serve the needs of others just as Jesus did."
RT HON. SIR JEFFREY DONALDSON MP

"How encouraging to read of the queen's faith in the Lord Jesus in her own words. I look forward to reading this inspiring biography with my grandchildren!"
MARY MOHLER, Author, *Growing in Gratitude*

"Packed full of fun facts, fascinating snippets of history and deeply moving extracts from the queen's speeches, this book manages to be both inspirational and informative."
LINDA ALLCOCK, Author, *Head, Heart, Hands* and *Deeper Still*

"This little book tells the story of a truly remarkable lady, Queen Elizabeth II, who has set a tremendous example in her Christian faith and is a role model for us all."
WILLIAM HUMPHREY MBE, MLA, President, North West Belfast District Scout Council; Chair, Northern Ireland Assembly Branch, Commonwealth Parliamentary Association

"Inspire your kids with the life of Queen Elizabeth II. This engaging story reveals her life ambition—to serve Jesus Christ, her 'Saviour' and 'anchor'."
BARBARA REAOCH, Author, *A Jesus Christmas* and *A Jesus Easter*

"A lovely, concise celebration of Queen Elizabeth and her faith!"
BOB HARTMAN, Author, *The Prisoners, the Earthquake and the Midnight Song*

Queen Elizabeth II
© The Good Book Company 2022. Reprinted 2022
Illustrated by Emma Randall | Design and Art Direction by André Parker
Series Concept by Laura Caputo-Wickham | Photography Credit: PolizeiBerlin
"The Good Book For Children" is an imprint of The Good Book Company Ltd.
thegoodbook.com | thegoodbook.co.uk | thegoodbook.com.au
thegoodbook.co.nz | thegoodbook.co.in
ISBN: 9781784987527 | Printed in Turkey

thegoodbook
for children

Do Great Things for God

Queen Elizabeth II

The Queen Who Chose to Serve

Alison Mitchell

Illustrated by Emma Randall

When Princess Elizabeth was born, nobody thought she would become queen!

Growing up with her sister, Margaret, she lived in a big house, but it wasn't a palace.

Elizabeth loved animals. She played with her father's corgis and was given her first horse, a Shetland pony named Peggy, when she was four.

It was a happy way to grow up. But then, when she was ten, everything changed...

Elizabeth's uncle, King Edward VIII, decided he didn't want to be king anymore. The whole country was astonished!

Suddenly Elizabeth's father was the king — King George VI — and Elizabeth knew she would become queen after him.

And now they did live in a palace —
Buckingham Palace in the middle of London.

In 1939, when Elizabeth was 13, World War II started. Buckingham Palace was bombed.

It wasn't safe so, like 600,000 other children in London, Elizabeth and Margaret moved away from the city.

Princess Elizabeth knew how scared many children must be, so in 1940 she gave her first public talk, on the BBC's *Children's Hour* on the radio.

"God will care for us,"
she said.

When she was 18, Elizabeth joined the Auxiliary Territorial Service, where she trained to be a driver and mechanic. That was such a surprising thing for the future queen to do that the British newspapers called her

"Princess Auto Mechanic".

When the war finished, Elizabeth and Margaret wanted
to join in with the celebrations in London, so they slipped
out of the palace to join the crowds. Elizabeth pulled her
cap down low — and no one recognised them!

In 1947, Elizabeth married Philip. They were visiting Kenya a few years later when everything changed again. Elizabeth's father, King George VI, died — so, aged 25, Elizabeth was queen!

On 2nd June 1953, Elizabeth was crowned. There were over 8,000 guests at the service, and huge crowds lined the streets as she went past.

Elizabeth was given the crown jewels to wear.

But they weren't the most precious thing she was given.

At one point in the service she was given

"the most valuable thing that this world affords*".

What was it? A Bible — God's word.

*"affords" means "gives"

Elizabeth was not just the queen of the UK.
She was also the head of over 50 other countries.

In the past, many of these nations had been part of
the British Empire. These countries are now part of the
Commonwealth of Nations, and the queen is its head.

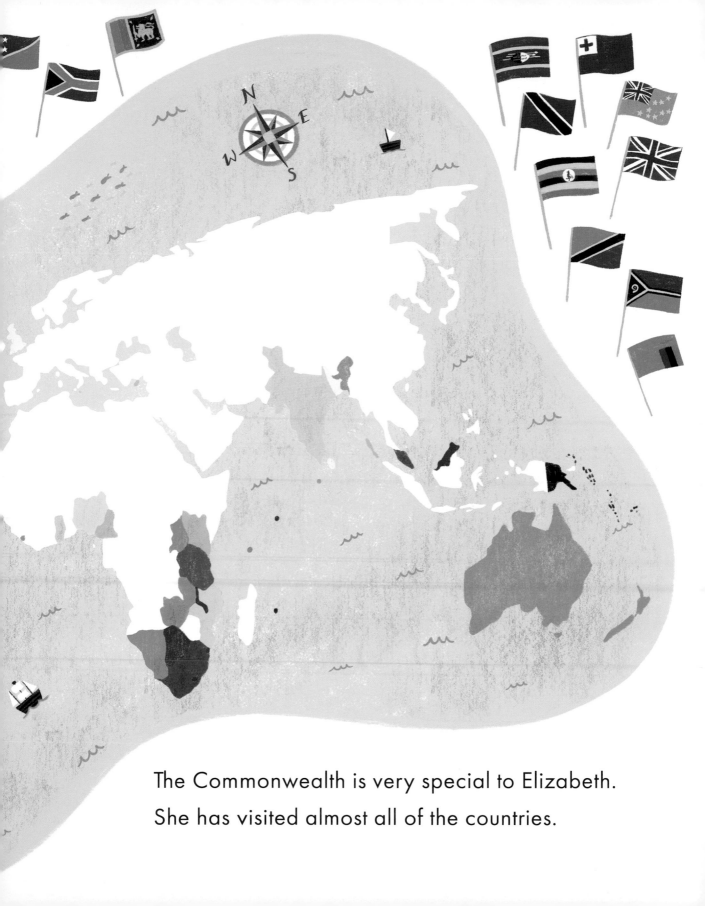

The Commonwealth is very special to Elizabeth.
She has visited almost all of the countries.

As well as visiting a lot of countries, the queen has met a lot of people.

Winston Churchill

John F. Kennedy

Margaret Thatcher

Kwame Nkrumah

The Beatles

She has met 14 British prime ministers and 13 American presidents — as well as pop stars, athletes and actors from across the world.

She also knew the Bible teachers
Billy Graham and John Stott.

Barack Obama

Tanni Grey-Thompson

David Beckham

The Spice Girls

Boris Johnson

But Elizabeth has met even more people
who weren't famous at all...

During her life, the queen has been "patron" of over 600 charities and organisations. Just as Elizabeth loves to serve others, so do the thousands of people she has met who are part of these charities.

Cancer Research UK

Girlguiding and Scout A...

The National Horse Racing Museum

BATTERSEA

Battersea Dogs and Cats Home

The Piobaireachd Society

The Boys' Brigade

The Bible Society

Being a queen must be wonderful in lots of ways, but it can also be hard. Queen Elizabeth is watched everywhere she goes, and people write all kinds of things about her and her family.

In 1992, so many hard things happened that Elizabeth called it her "annus horribilis", which is Latin for "horrible year". Her grown-up children were going through lots of difficulties. And there was a huge fire at her home in Windsor Castle. Over 100 rooms were destroyed.

But whether it's been a good year or a bad year, there is one thing that the queen has always done. Every Christmas Day, at 3pm, she has given a speech, and millions and millions of people in the UK and Commonwealth have turned their TVs on to watch.

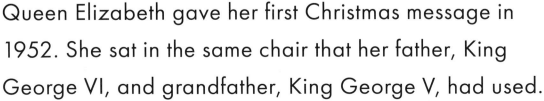

Queen Elizabeth gave her first Christmas message in 1952. She sat in the same chair that her father, King George VI, and grandfather, King George V, had used.

"Pray for me," she said, "... that God may give me wisdom and strength to carry out the solemn promises I shall be making, and that I may faithfully serve him and you, all the days of my life".

The queen has often talked about her Christian faith in her Christmas messages. Here are some of the things she has said:

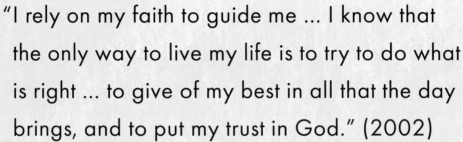

"I rely on my faith to guide me ... I know that the only way to live my life is to try to do what is right ... to give of my best in all that the day brings, and to put my trust in God." (2002)

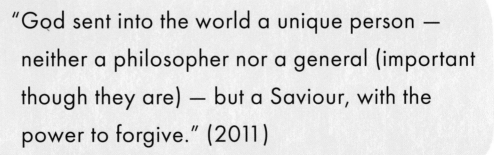

"God sent into the world a unique person — neither a philosopher nor a general (important though they are) — but a Saviour, with the power to forgive." (2011)

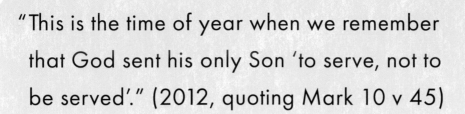

"This is the time of year when we remember that God sent his only Son 'to serve, not to be served'." (2012, quoting Mark 10 v 45)

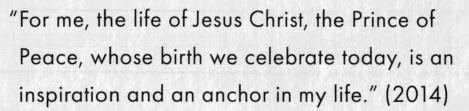

"For me, the life of Jesus Christ, the Prince of Peace, whose birth we celebrate today, is an inspiration and an anchor in my life." (2014)

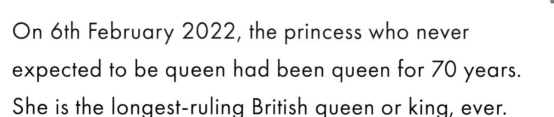

On 6th February 2022, the princess who never expected to be queen had been queen for 70 years. She is the longest-ruling British queen or king, ever.

For Queen Elizabeth, Jesus Christ has been her "Saviour" and her "anchor". She has chosen to serve him all of her life.

Queen Elizabeth II

1926 Princess Elizabeth Alexandra Mary was born on the 21st of April. Although her grandfather was King George V, her father was the king's younger son, meaning Elizabeth was never expected to become queen.

1936 Elizabeth's uncle, King Edward VIII, abdicated. Suddenly, Elizabeth's father became King George VI.

1939 When Elizabeth was 13, World War II broke out. In 1940, Buckingham Palace was bombed, so Elizabeth and her sister, Margaret, were evacuated from London. Their parents stayed in Buckingham Palace to show solidarity with those living through the London Blitz.

1944 Elizabeth joined the ATS (Auxiliary Territorial Service) when she turned 18. She trained to be a driver and mechanic.

1947 Elizabeth married Prince Philip on the 20th of November. They lived in Malta for two years while Philip served as an officer in the Royal Navy.

1952 King George VI died on the 6th of February, and Elizabeth became queen. Her coronation on the 2nd of June 1953 was attended by 8,000 guests, with crowds of 3 million in the streets, and watched by 20 million people on television. As well as becoming the British queen, Elizabeth was now the head of the Commonwealth of Nations.

1957 Elizabeth gave her first televised Christmas message.

1977 Britain celebrated the queen's Silver Jubilee (25 years as monarch). Millions celebrated with street parties across Britain. There have been similar celebrations for her Golden (2002) and Diamond (2012) Jubilees.

2022 On the 6th of February 2022, Elizabeth celebrated 70 years as queen (her Platinum Jubilee). She is Britain's longest-serving monarch.

Queen Elizabeth has seen many world-changing events since her coronation in 1953. She has also worked with 14 British prime ministers and has met every US president since Harry S. Truman (except for President Lyndon B. Johnson). The queen's travels have taken her to over 110 countries across six continents, making her Britain's best-travelled as well as longest-reigning monarch. During this time she has also been patron of more than 600 charities and organisations across the UK and the Commonwealth.

Her Majesty Queen Elizabeth II

"For even the Son of Man [Jesus] did not
come to be served, but to serve, and to
give his life as a ransom for many."
Mark 10 v 45